D0459728

1997
REC'D
)98
)

1998

)9
)9
) 2000

ART CENTER COLLEGE OF DESIGN LIBRARY
1700 LIDA STREET
PASADENA, CALIFORNIA 91103

ART CENTER COLLEGE OF DESIGN

3 3220 00098 6898

ART CENTER COLLEGE OF DESIGN LIBRARY
1700 LIDA STREET
PASADENA, CALIFORNIA 91103

760
T564h
c.2

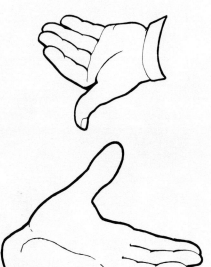

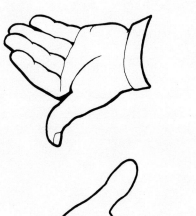
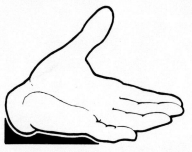

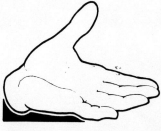

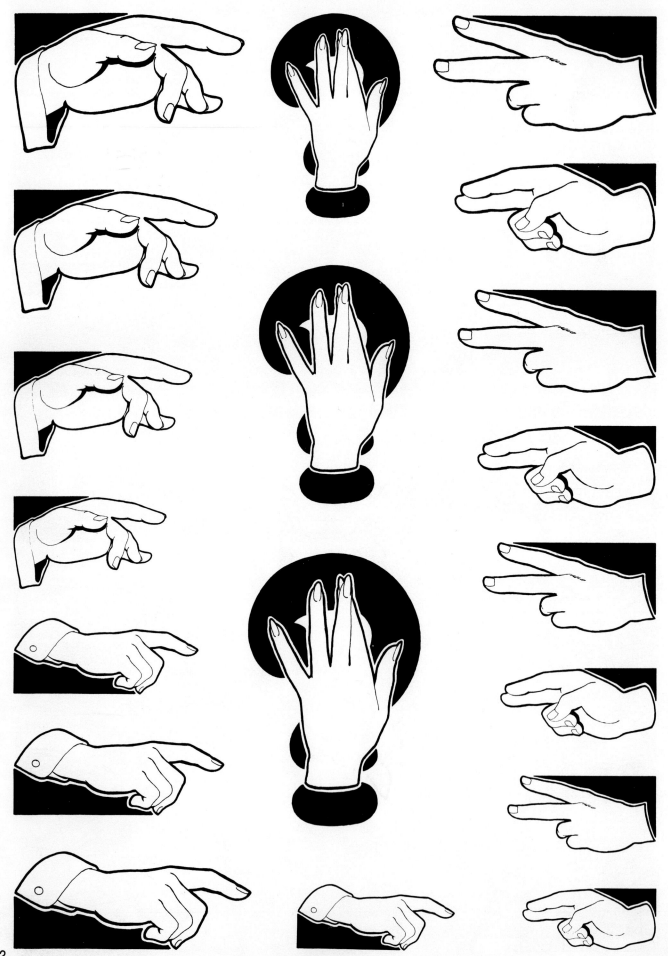

2

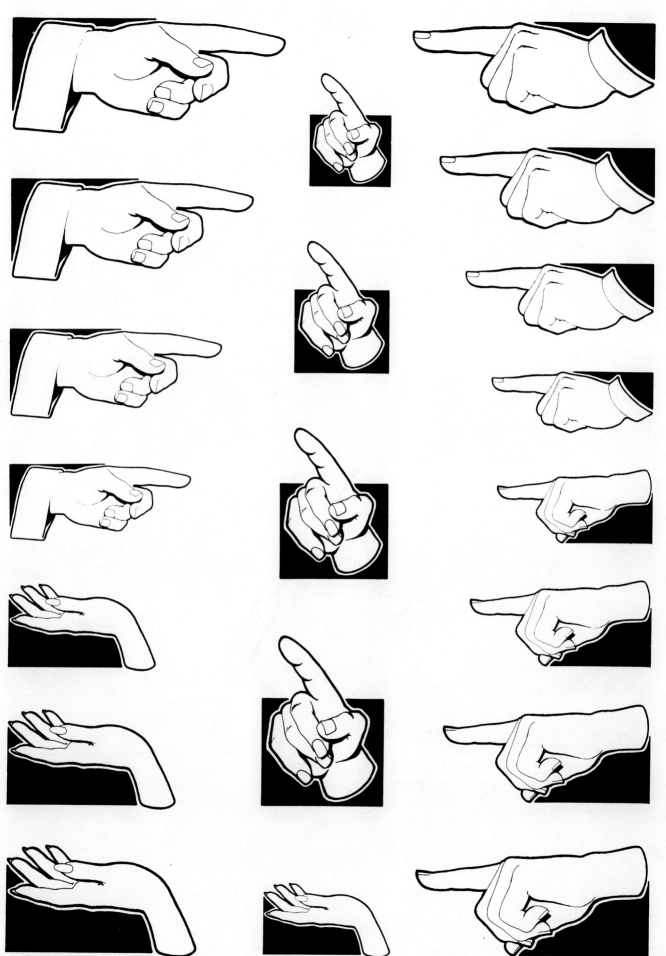

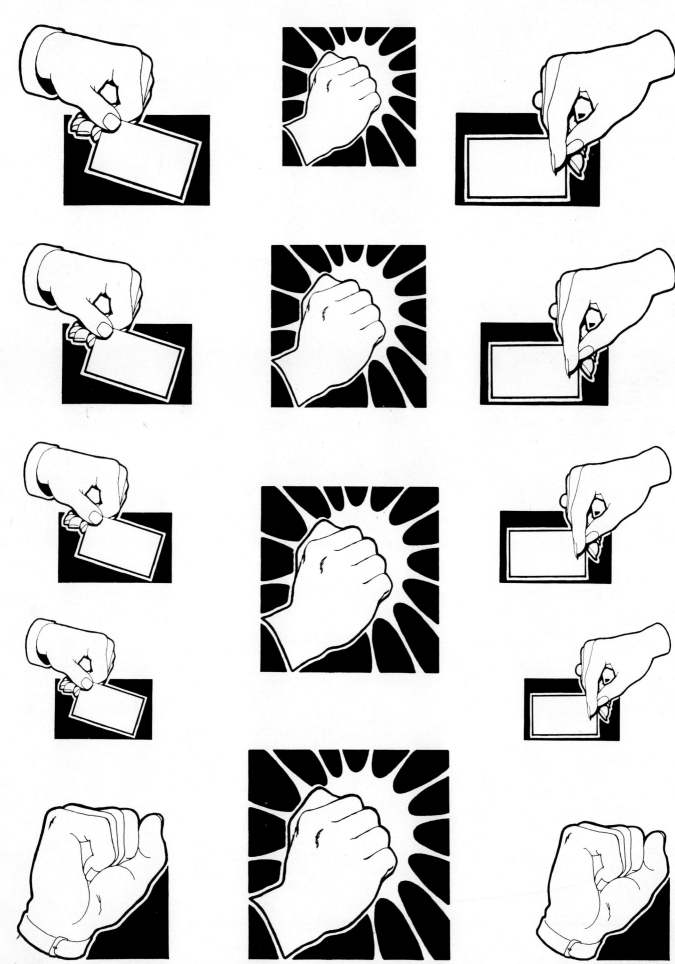

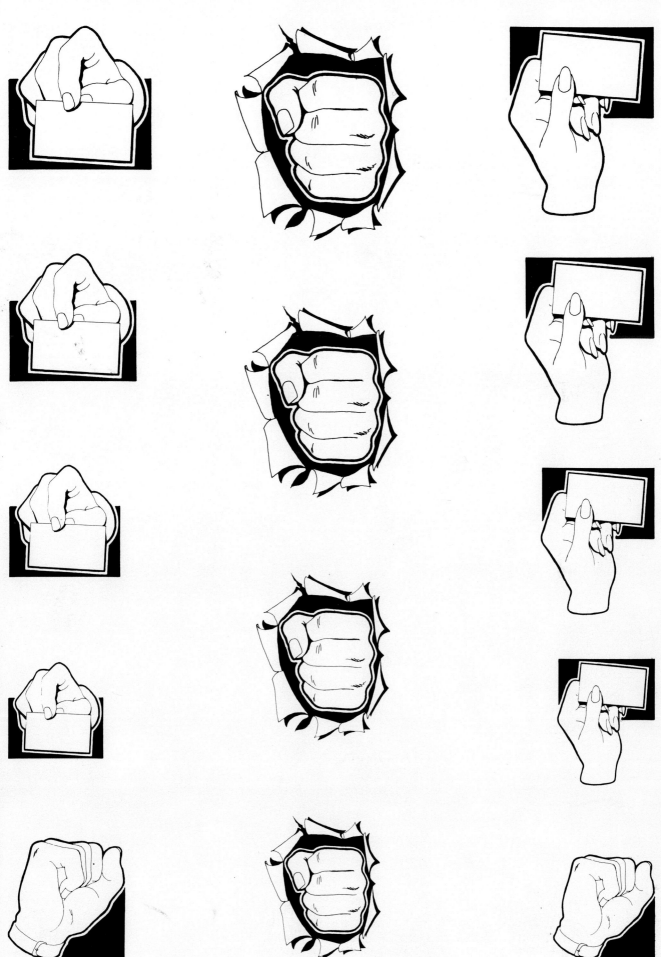

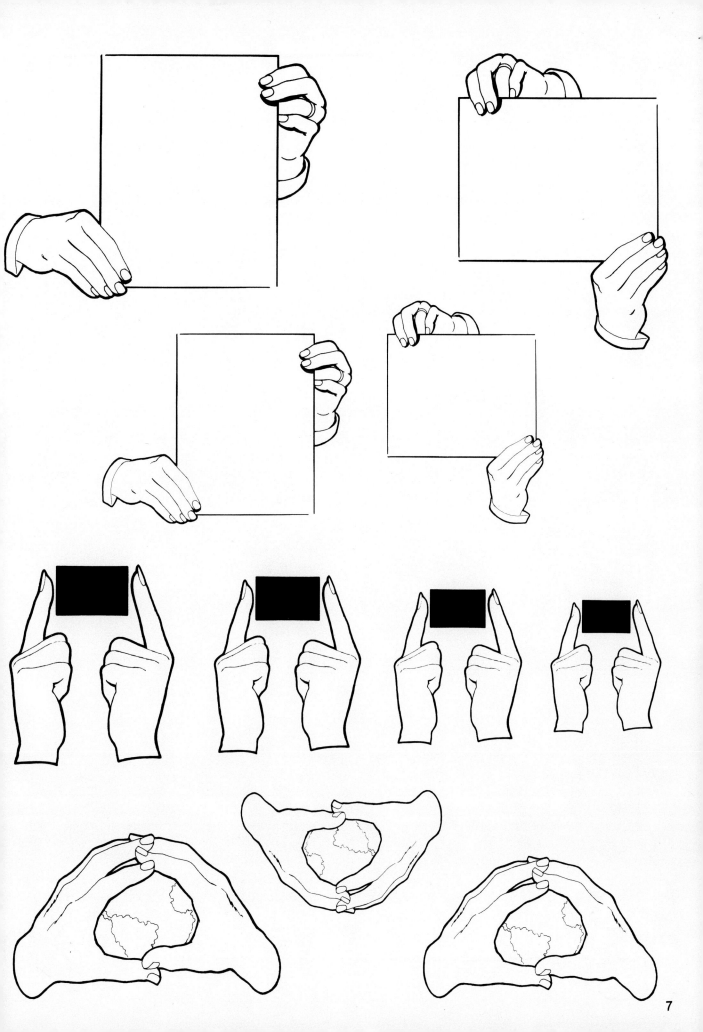

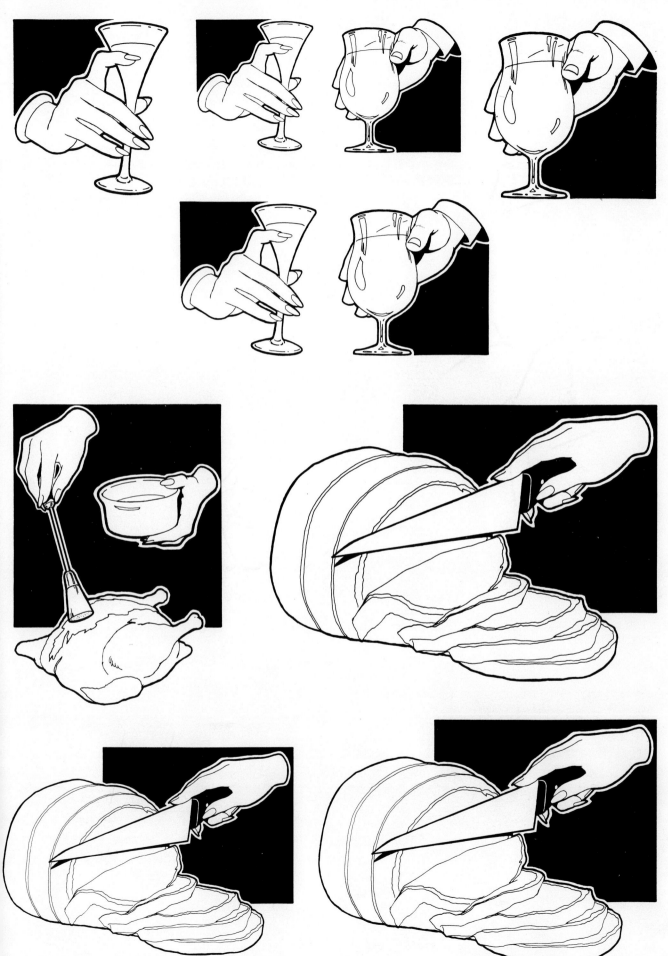

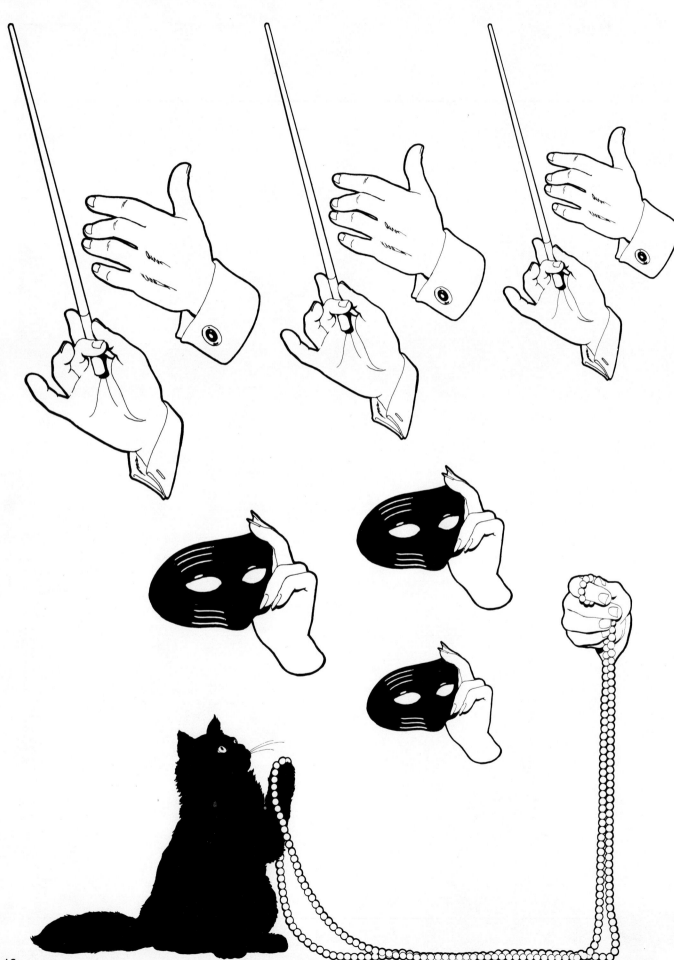

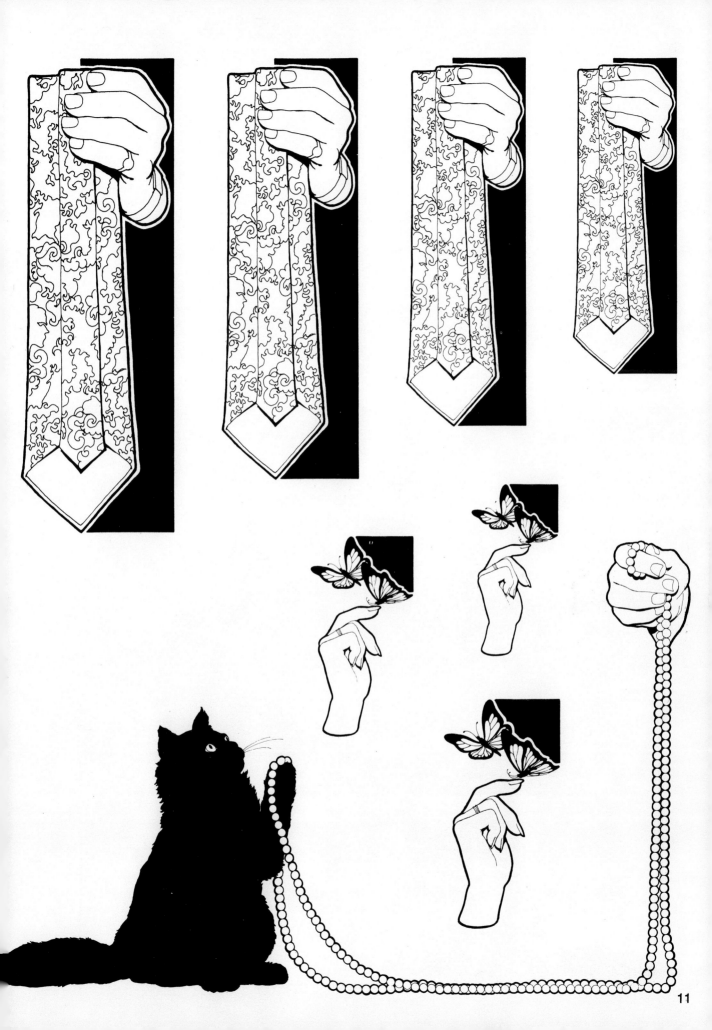

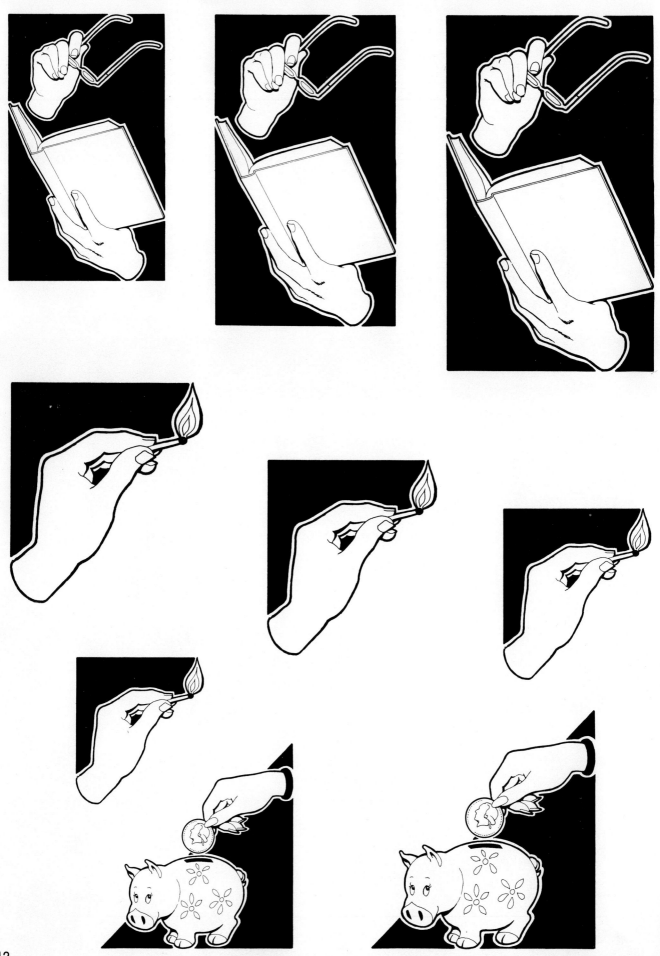

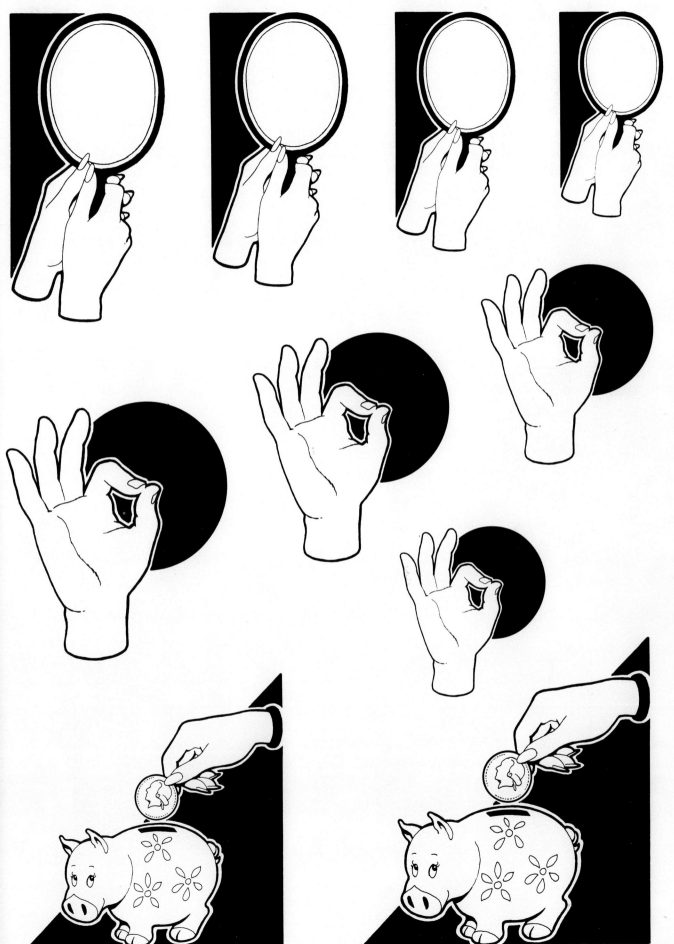

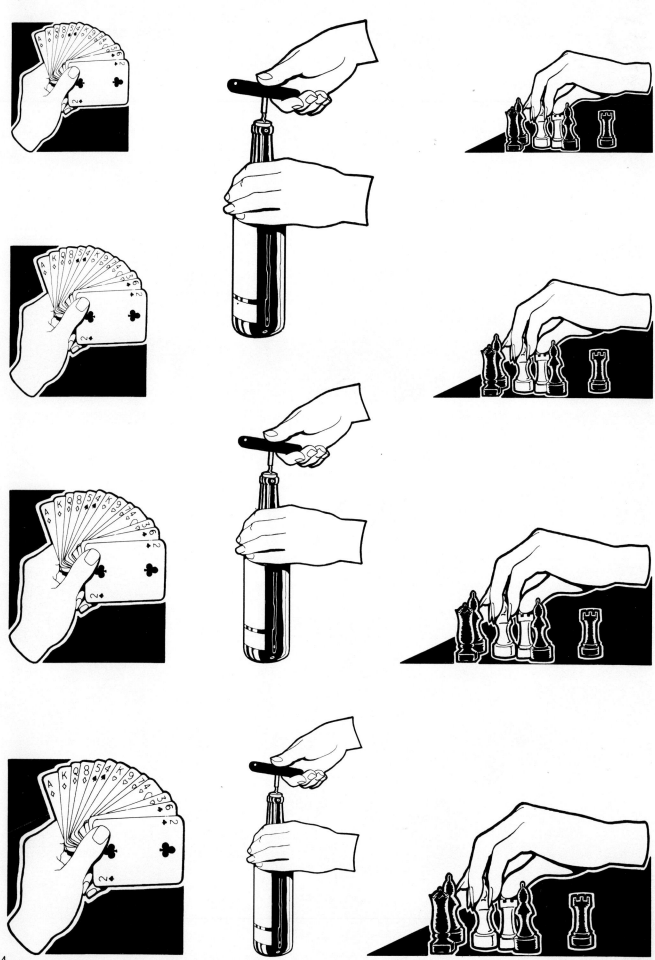

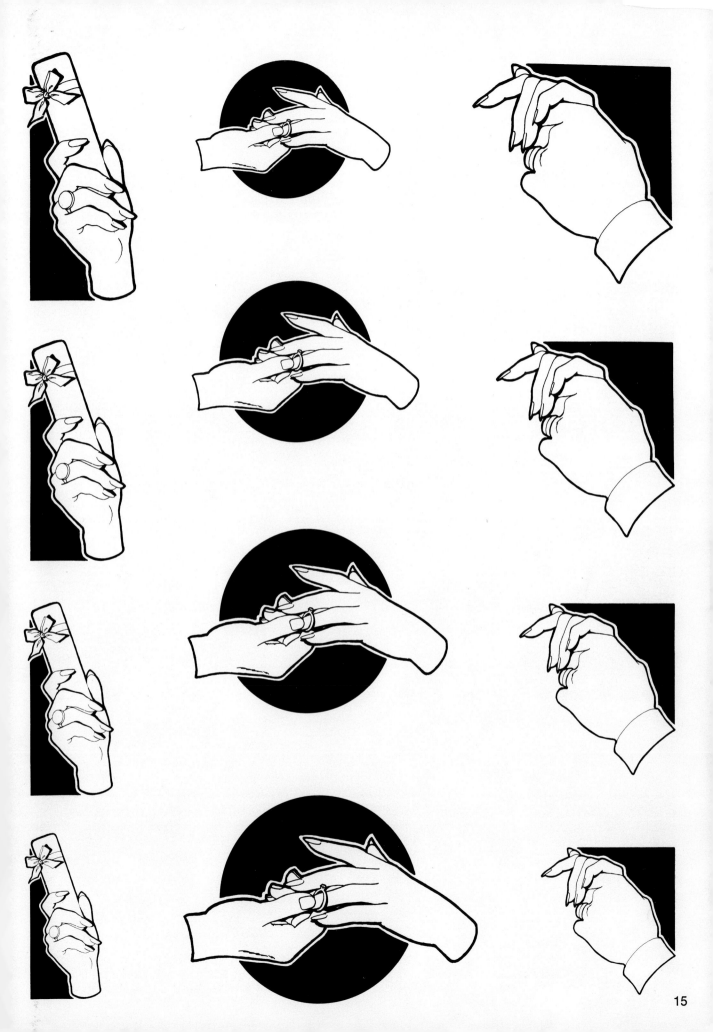

15

ART CENTER COLLEGE OF DESIGN LIBRARY
1700 LIDA STREET
PASADENA, CALIFORNIA 91103

17

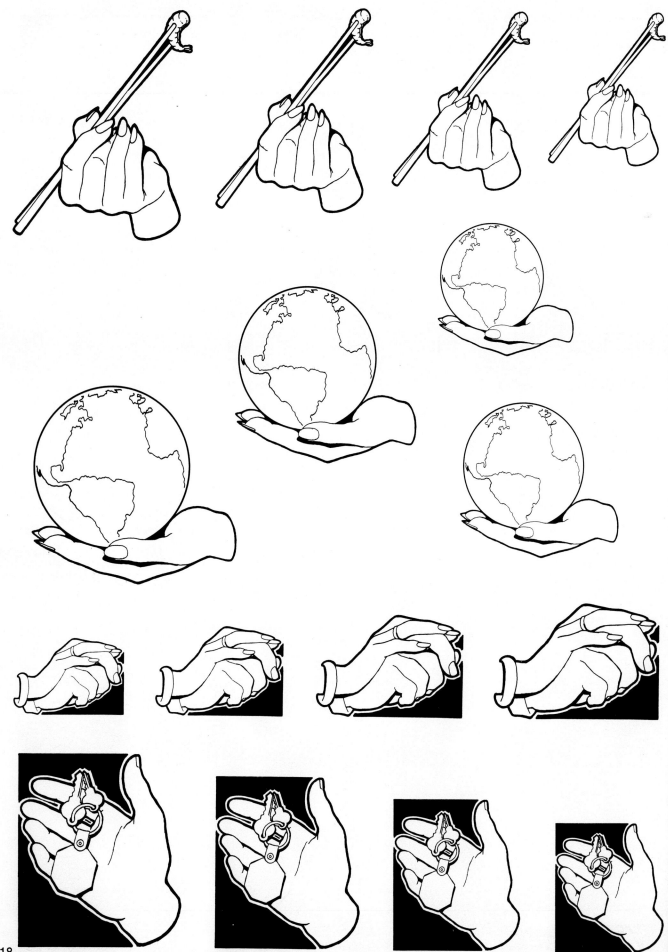

18

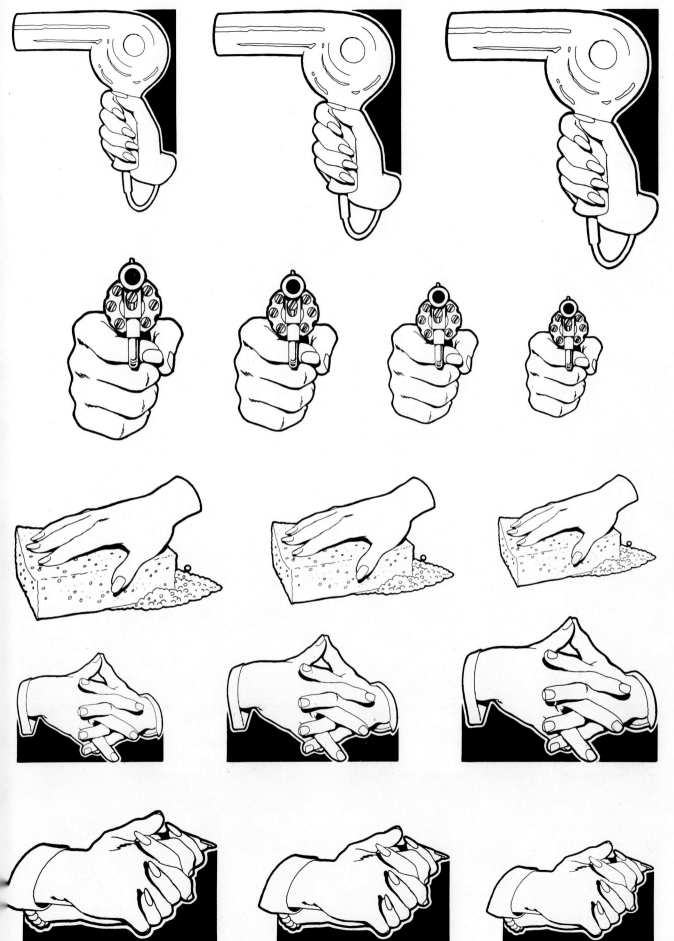

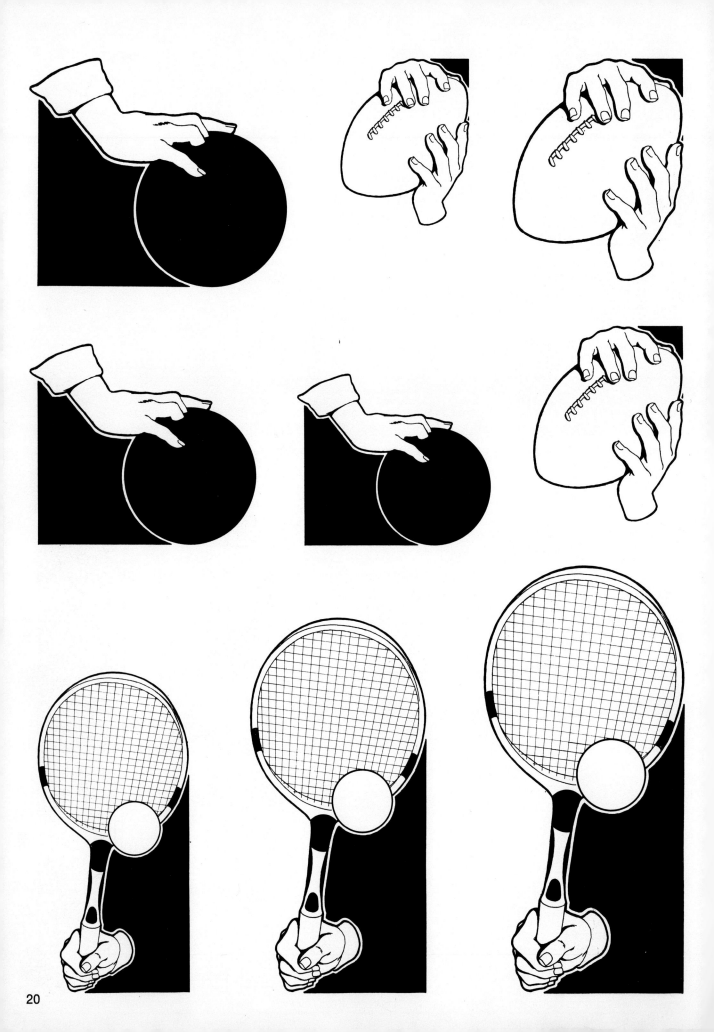

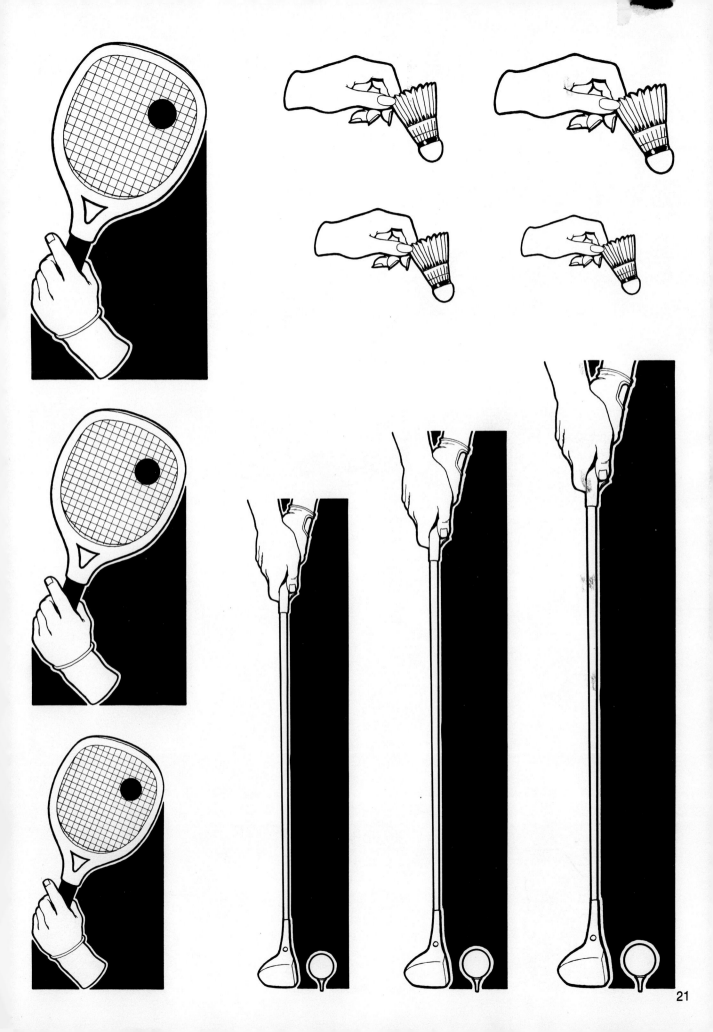

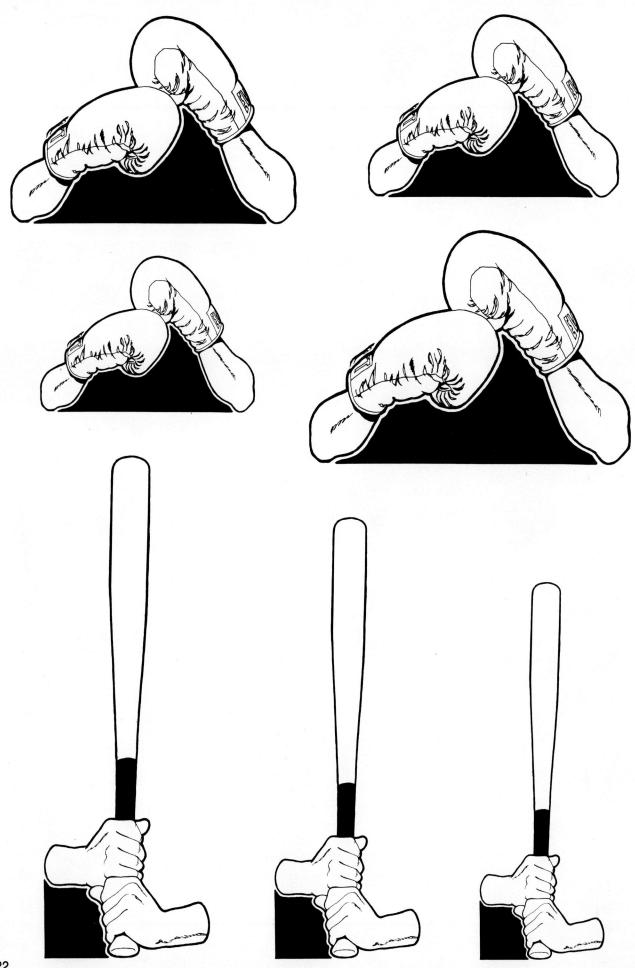

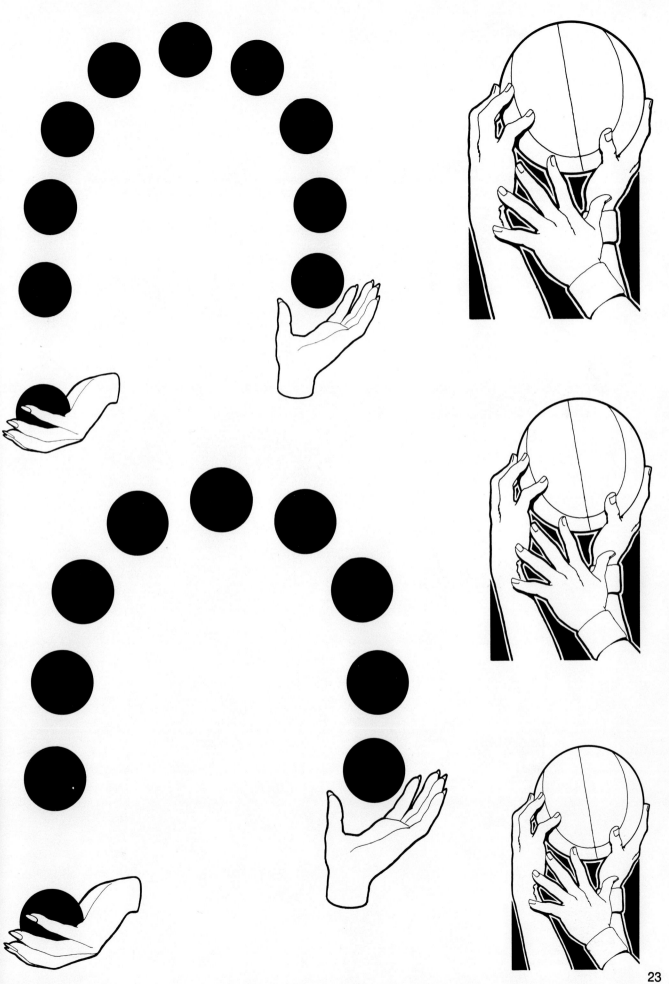

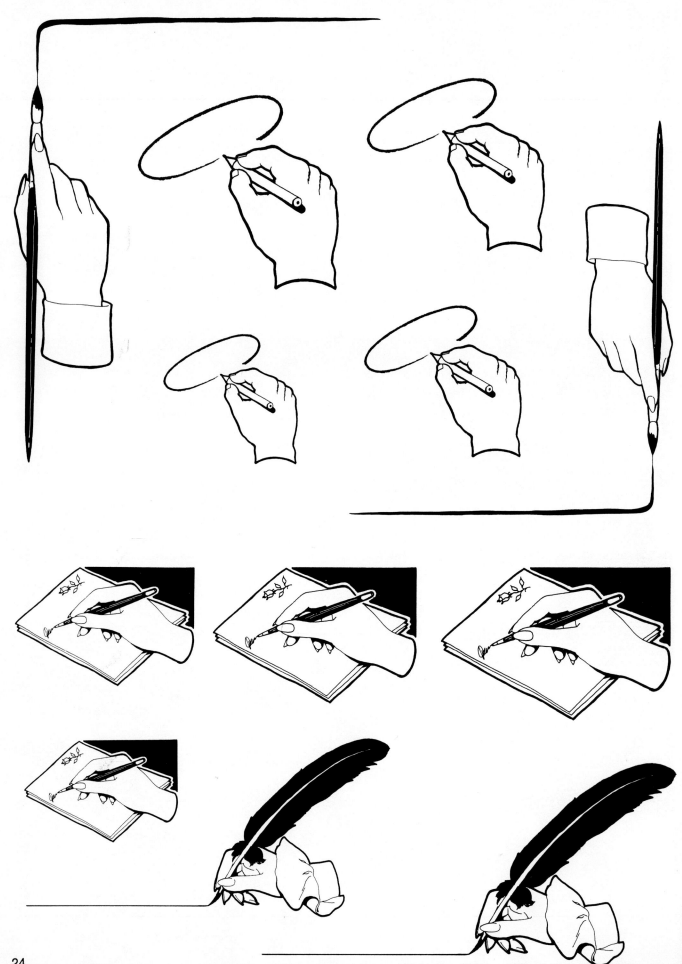

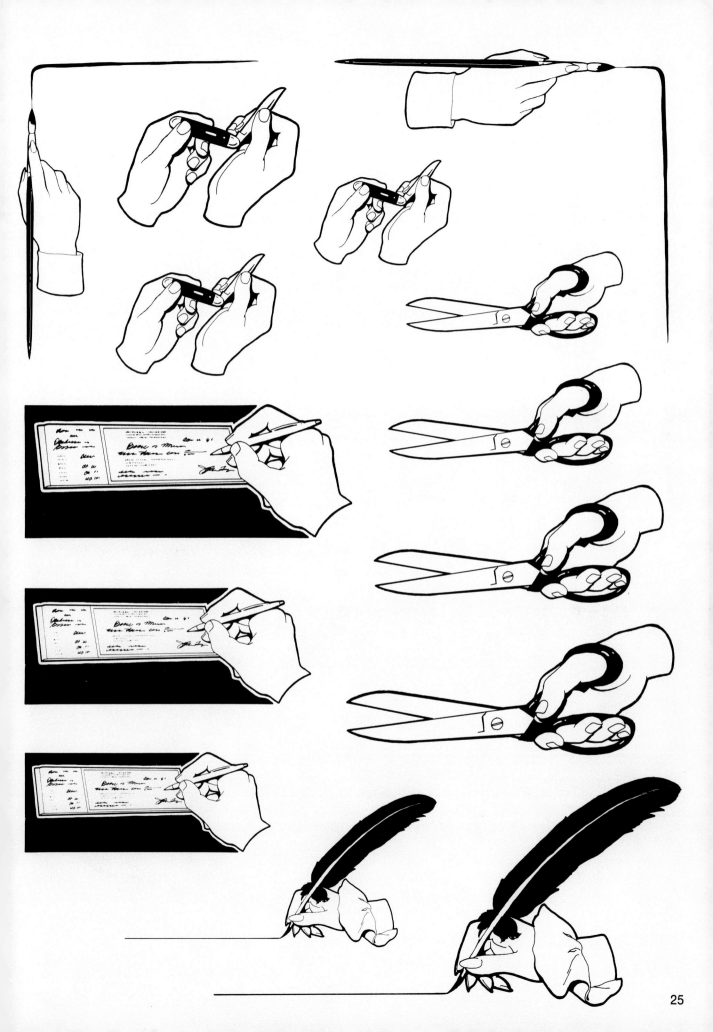

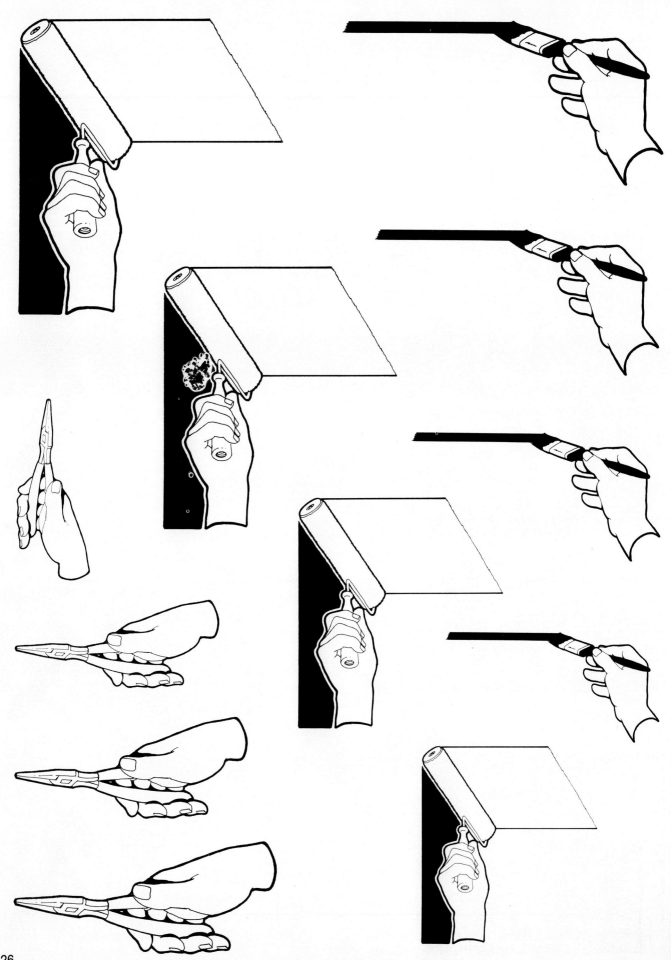

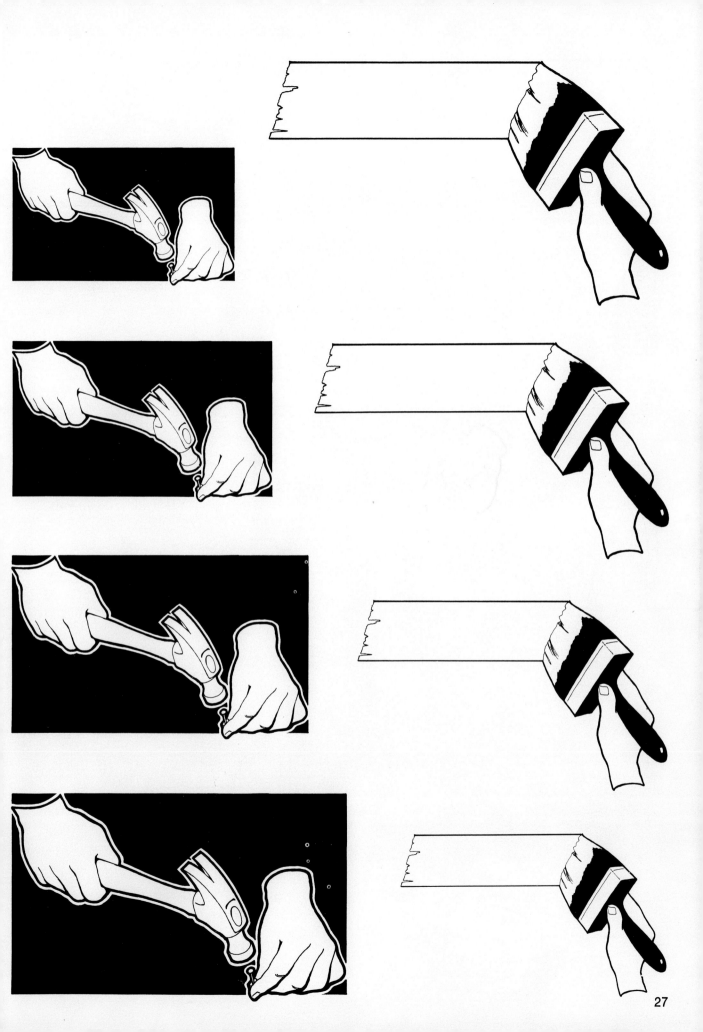

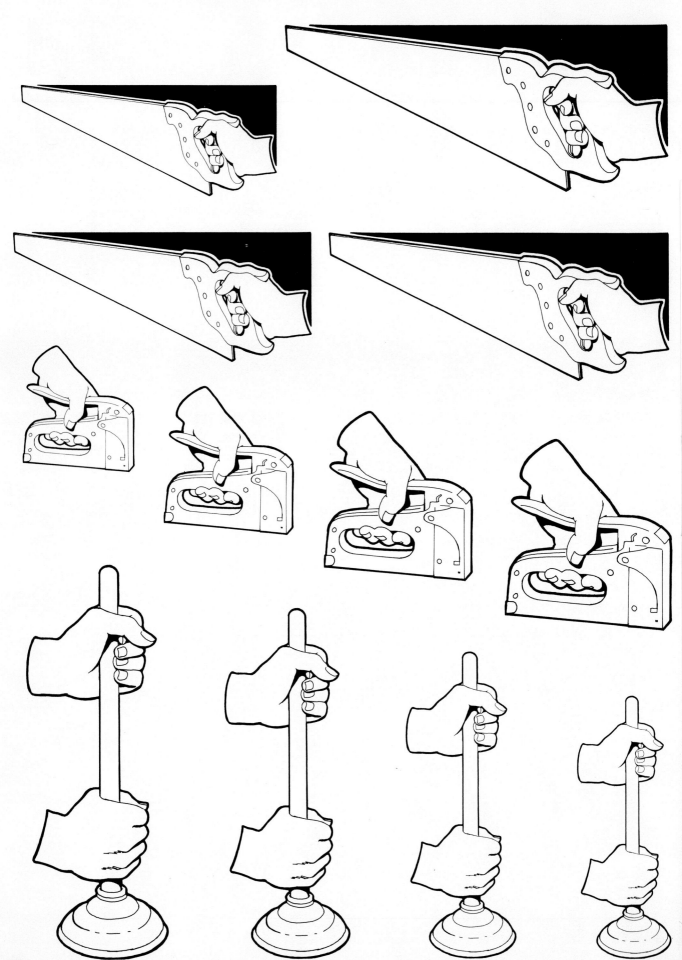

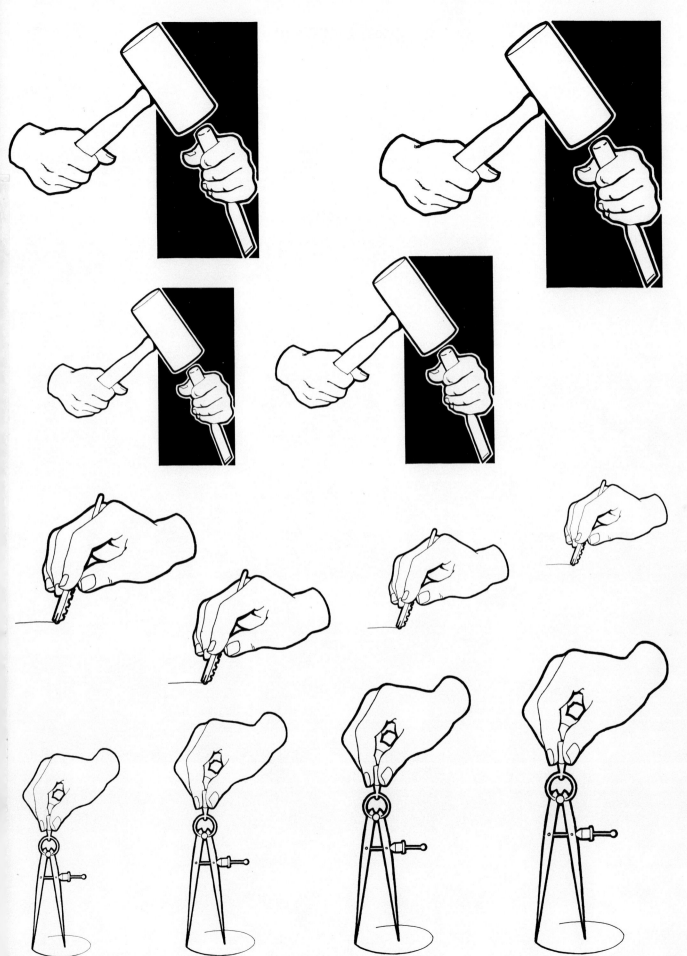

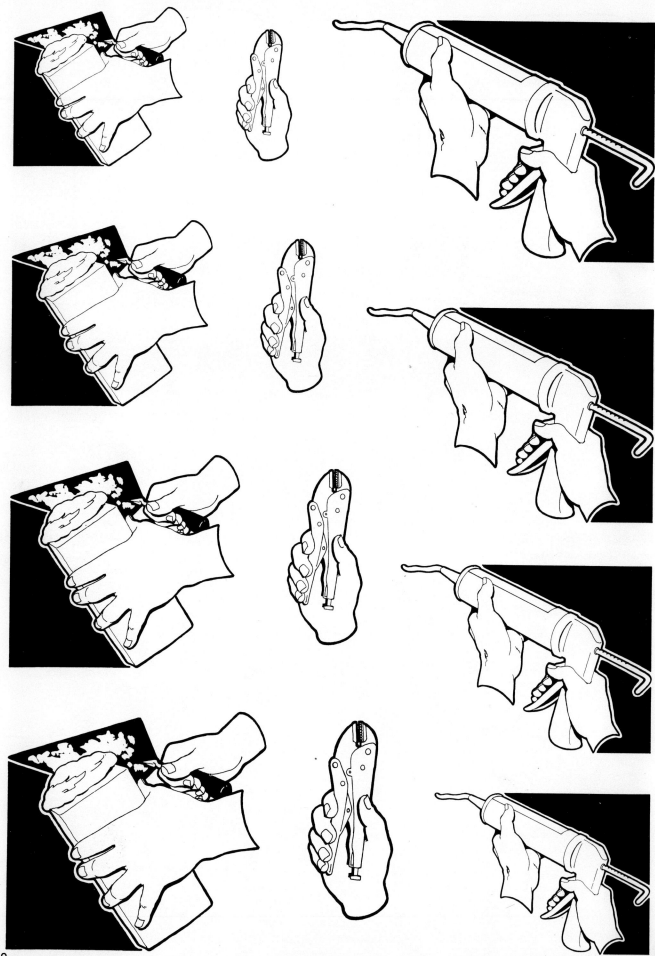

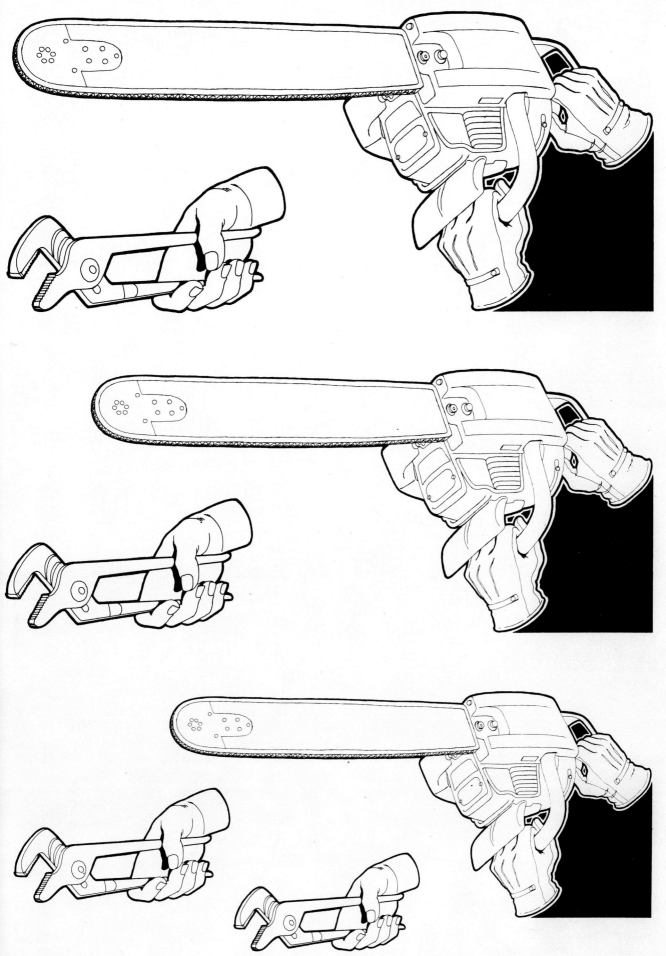

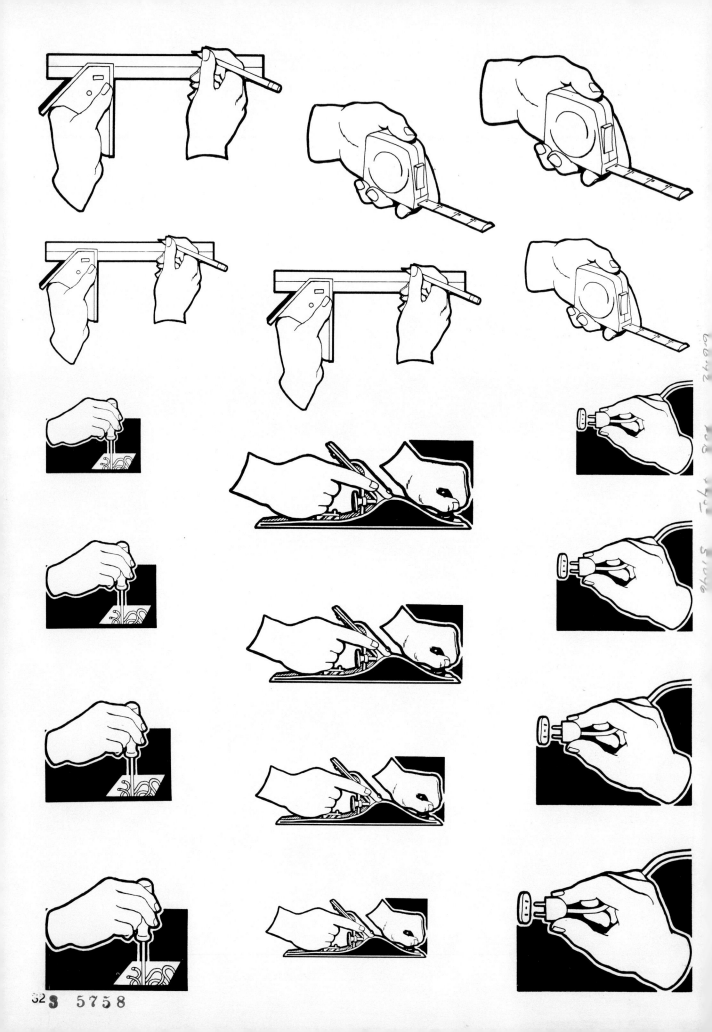

 § 5758

60984 81800

575 6690
1183 rn. Olympic (0 Shrin Eastmum Lobby Level Test
310 - 753 - 3600
Hilba to Loghe (0 wast
ch Barby E. Olympic